Introduction

A collection of 50+ messages for coaches, all gleaned from a forty year involvement with Gaelic Football. Not every lesson was learned at the time it should have been. Some took years to get through. Others were lightbulb moments. This book is for coaches who are always seeking to improve their own skills and the skills of others. The content is set out in short, bitesize passages. Whether you coach GAA or another team sport, there's something in here for you. A few hints on what to expect:

There are many reasons for a player being slow to make decisions on the ball.
Not every player who disengages is lazy.
There are players who like to be challenged.
Peer mentoring can be more powerful than coach talk.
Coached attacking play does not deny players opportunities to be creative.
Creating teamplayers isn't as difficult as it used to be.
Team selection is a minefield, but doesn't have to be.
We all have a default coaching method and it's tough to let go.
Handovers can be perfect springboards for further development.
A slick training session may not be a good sign.
Disciplined play doesn't only apply to defending.

Cover photo courtesy of Vecteezy.com

BITESIZE LESSONS FROM COACHING

1. There are many reasons for a player being slow to make decisions on the ball.
2. Making good decisions off the ball can be tough.
3. There are players who only pass to certain teammates..and they have their reasons.
4. Some conversations about fitness are taboo.
5. Not every player who disengages is lazy.
6. The player with a sideline parent/coach needs the club to step up.
7. There are players who like to be challenged… and others who have yet to find out that they do too.
8. Some players are serial complainers and may not know it.
9. There are those who learn best when given a choice.
10. If you spot a player who finds it difficult to mix with teammates, find out more.
11. When you discover a player who is an innovator, have regular conversations.
12. Evasion often fails due to one tiny detail.
13. Peer mentoring can be more powerful than coach talk.

14. Make sure you understand the true meaning of readiness.
15. Settle only for the appropriate equipment and plenty of it.
16. Getting coach:player ratios right is a major plus.
17. Try not to rely on others for access to facilities.
18. Coaching bilateral skills can be a long litany of dietary lapses.
19. Changes of pace are serious weapons we may not use enough.
20. Drills and Games – look for an ideal balance.
21. Coaching isn't as much about variety nowadays.
22. Coached attacking play does not deny players opportunities to be creative.
23. Defensive coaching can be confusing.
24. Sooner or later I was bound to focus on coaching the individual (PDC).
25. Creating teamplayers isn't as difficult as it used to be.
26. Position rotation is a great way for players to learn.
27. TACOS is an easy way to plan kickouts and give everyone a role.
28. Getting to know players is not a bonus…it's a must.
29. Team selection is a minefield, but doesn't have to be.

30. One of the best things you can do is assign coaching roles to selectors and mentors.
31. We all have a default coaching method and it's tough to let go.
32. It makes sense for coaches to learn sideline roles and responses.
33. Team talks are best left to one true orator.
34. Feedback can be an acquired taste.
35. 'In game' changes mean different things to different people.
36. The most successful coach recruiters do house calls.
37. Parental contact is all about updating and educating.
38. What players hear from coaches must be clear, encouraging and agreed.
39. Communication between different age groups is largely absent.
40. Handovers can be perfect springboards for further development.
41. S&C has its place...and that place is right at the heart of player development.
42. We need more role models to highlight the importance of proper nutrition and hydration.
43. Video recording and analysis are no longer the preserve of adult teams.
44. Let it run, let it run, let it run....respond.
45. Awkward but effective = leave it be.
46. If an engine isn't running smoothly...
47. Supporting roles can be difficult to master.

48. A slick training session may not be a good sign.
49. Does the playing area suit what you want to do?
50. To pass or not to pass….that is the question.
51. The days of feeding the ball into a 6v6 are gone.
52. There's an attacking acronym to help with specifics.
53. If you feel you need to be vocal, try commentating instead of instructing.
54. Disciplined play doesn't only apply to defending.
55. And finally….adding to a library of stuff will never be as important as learning how best to use it.

1
There are many reasons for a player being slow to make decisions on the ball.

Different players have different stumbling blocks. Among the more common are….

The player who lacks confidence performing the technical skills and may need all of his concentration to execute these. For him, the idea of responding to calls from teammates is way down his list of priorities. He's already spinning three plates; he doesn't have time for a fourth. He will tend to offload the ball without looking for options…simply because his focus is elsewhere. An obvious priority for the coach is to help this player improve his technical skills, scaffolding learning.

Having said that, trying to improve technique while seeking better decision-making in training games can be a bridge too far for many. One way to prioritise decision-making is to promote a way of playing that many will view as a restriction or denial, rather than something positive. Take away one of the more difficult skills….**solo running**….and replace it with a single bounce. Do not be tempted to add a toe-tap, just to make it a two-touch play. The solo run may well be a unique selling point for Gaelic football, but this player doesn't need it. He will benefit much more from a **'four steps, bounce, four steps, pass/shoot'** approach (or a shortened version of it).

Next, the player who can control the ball quite well in open space but who hesitates when others (including teammates) enter that space, even when they are still far enough away to not have any influence. This is the player who has run into contact and lost out so many times in the past that he now puts the brakes on quicker than needed and offloads the ball with a short hand pass, usually a lateral one. His pass is generally accurate, so there's no need to push for wholesale change.

One way to sidestep this issue is to link him with a teammate who usually plays ahead of him on the pitch. You don't need to announce this to anyone other than the link player. Allow them time to work together. It's all about giving the poor decision-maker a focus….a target that will blur the other bodies and help him to learn when and where to play the ball towards his teammate.

Finally, the technically gifted player who has all the weaponry to keep the ball off one or more opponents, jinking this way and that, doubling back and toe-tapping on the spot as if he is choosing from a menu of disposal options. This is the player who feigns scanning and throws an arm out to signal that nobody ahead of him is moving. If you have one of these at your club, let him see this message:

"Nobody ahead is moving because they're tired moving now. You haven't looked for them!"

2
Making good decisions off the ball can be tough.

Here are two 'off the ball' situations to consider.
The first is when the player doesn't have the ball, but his team does. The second is when the opposition has it.

Off the ball movement grabs our attention when our team is on the attack.
Who is making a move to receive a pass?
Who is running to make room for teammates?
Is the player changing pace or direction or both?
Are the runs well-timed?
These are all worth observing and acting upon, if necessary.
But there's something else that permeates underage and youth football; **no run at all.**
It covers anything from standing to walking to jogging, but with no conviction. This player is lost.
He has no idea of where to run, when to run and even why to run. Unless you struggle for numbers, this player is not one of the starting team…..yet!
He presents a challenge and that's why you should accept it. Without help, this player will not learn how best to act when his team is attacking.
He needs a mentor. Don't waste time asking him where he thinks he should run or why he runs to places that are not useful. That's like a mechanic asking me to fit a cylinder head gasket; there will be no response.

Strip the game back for the player and let him sample a variety of runs, overseen by you, his mentor. Let him know that learning may take time, mistakes will be plentiful and that you are both aiming to make small improvements rather than huge leaps. Observing and copying can really help here.

Your player doesn't always need to be active. He may pick up more from watching someone play, so find a good example to illustrate. If you use a full forward to point out the way he runs away laterally from in front of goal (to make room for others), then don't wait long before giving your player his chance to copy that one move.

Remove all other duties from him….and don't add a second and third demand while he learns to time and properly pace that run away from the middle. After he has made the move, let him rejoin the game as he sees fit. Once he has mastered the run, asking him questions will probably elicit a better response than if he had been asked before he got the hang of it.

"Ok…so you've made the run to this point and your opponent has come with you.
What might be happening in the middle area now?
If your team scores, how will you have contributed to that score?"

Add in another layer to further challenge the player. Look for incremental gains. The same message applies to whatever you would like this player to learn. Too many tasks and the need to make several linked decisions have proved to be his undoing in the past. Unburden him and let him develop.

Quite the opposite of this is the player who wants the ball at every opportunity and generally runs at pace towards the ball carrier, already yelling his war cry.... *"Yeah, yeah, yeah, yeah!"* Regardless of what's happening around him, he's there to take the ball and that's it. Yes, there are times when an offload to this player will be the better choice, but there are many more times when any other option is preferable.

The player (and we all know at least one) will probably be one of the the best solo runners on the team, blessed with the balance and agility of a black run skier. Unfortunately he may also have the attention span of a fruit fly! Working with him to develop a different playing style is an altogether different prospect.

His game is based on industry without thought. Standing still or running away from the ball are both non-starters for him. You'll need to present him with a portfolio of evidence to get him to take anything on board. Stats, video clips, peer comments etc are all ways to address this; yes, he will respond to constraints in training games, but learning may disappear like snow off a ditch when a particular restriction on him is eased. You may have to resort to applying the same constraints in competition games or for parts of them, at least.

When the opposition has the ball, decision-making may actually be a little easier, because so many coaches are giving players set defending positions and specific roles in those positions.

"If we lose the ball, drop back inside the 45."
"Get back immediately to protect the D."
"If you're in a wide position, tuck in to this part of the pitch. No point staying wide. They won't score from out there."
"If you lose the ball, your job is to chase it to win it back. Don't worry about covering. Others will be doing that."

Coaches have become much more prescriptive with regard to what they want from players when defending. The range of options is limited and that tends to help with decision-making. The player who is slow to make up his mind is likely to feel better because he is part of a defending package where everyone has to buy in.

3
There are players who only pass to certain teammates and they have their reasons.

Once again...two examples at either end of the spectrum.

> *The player who chooses to ignore some teammates, regardless of perceived advantage.*
> *The player who appears pressured into passing immediately to the closest teammate.*

Your first reaction may be as mine was for a long time.... confront the former and coach the latter.
Experience often tells us to look before we leap. In other words, find out more about the situations and the people before stepping in. Ask questions rather than make statements.

Let's take the player who chooses not to pass to certain teammates. He may indeed be giving the ball to a core group, all with skill levels which appear akin to his own.
Is he aware that he does this?
Is it deliberate?
If so, why?
Is it a trust issue?
Has he become frustrated with some players?
Was the ball being lost too often?

What appears to be happening may not be true. Gather the stats to establish facts. Be sure of your ground before opening a conversation. Very often, asking questions will lead to the player engaging. His answers may not match your thoughts, but that's where shifting the focus comes in. Chat about the player who hasn't been getting passes.
Is there a need to have others deliberately bring him into the game in training?
Might he benefit from some 1 to 1 coaching?
How may your experienced player help?

The one approach that has the least chance of effecting any change is confrontation. Even if the stats support the notion that he has been avoiding playing passes, your player is likely to go on the defensive, invoke the help of his core group and ask his own questions, such as.....

Would you pass to him?
It's not my job to improve him. Why is he no better than last year?
Do you want a score or do you want the ball to come straight back out for them to counter-attack?

There are no winners if it gets to this point.

Now...what about the player who appears to be pressured into passing to the closest teammate?

More often than not, this pass will come as a shock to both ball player and receiver. It's the hot potato pass. Typically, your passer will lack composure.
You may have heard the expression..
"All his troubles begin when he gets the ball."
There are so many reasons why this player may lack confidence. Perhaps he has poor technical skills; he may be comparing himself to others and thinking that you are doing that too. Previous mistakes on the ball may have led to these lightning offloads, with a fear of failure (or even contact) being ever present.

Whatever the case, there is still a reason not to jump in and help him as you see fit. He deserves the same chat time as the choosy passer you've just been reading about. He needs to know you value his opinion too. A conversation may bring clarity.
Is he keen to add to his skills?
Is he aware of his habits on the ball?
How can you help?
What can he do to help himself?
What if he tells you that he's happy doing what he's doing?

Take time to find out more before planning a way through.

4
Some conversations about fitness are taboo

We watch a player participate in training games and he looks the part when he has the ball; deft touches, scanning for possibilities and picking out teammates with accurate passes.
All is good until he has to move quickly and over a distance to receive the ball, to tackle an opponent or to add cover to the defence. He struggles to get there. What's holding him back?

At first glance, it appears that body shape could be a factor. He's not as wiry as his teammates. To the untrained eye, he looks to be carrying some excess weight.
Could it be diet?
Might these training sessions be his only exercise in a typical week?
Is he playing Xbox or PlayStation for hours each day?
These are a few of the go-to reasons that spring to mind. They are fuelled by media reports, research conducted by medical professionals and health bodies....and they are all valid. We accept them when they are presented as part of a national headline, but it's a different story when it comes to a named person in the club.

Firstly, one or more of the above reasons may be true; but how are coaches supposed to address the issue?

Secondly, we may be way off the mark and it may not be perceived as a problem at all.

Speaking with player and parent about a sedentary lifestyle is a much easier conversation than one about diet. The parent will often side with the coach when it comes to chats about the amount of screen time and the detrimental effects it can bring. Not so when diet is mentioned. Unless the player or parent broaches the subject, chances are it won't be mentioned. We may paint a picture in our heads of fizzy drinks, fast food and plenty of both. We may want to hear admissions in order to offer advice and a menu of options. But it's not going to happen, at least not in the vast majority of cases.

Strangely enough, some people who rail against any mention of a player being overweight are often quite happy to identify another as being far too thin and needing to start eating to build himself up.
"You need to put him in a grow bag" cannot be considered acceptable, just as *"You need to sit him away from the table"* is not.

So...back to our player who has problems covering the ground. One way to get a parent and player on board is to have a chat with both about **a move towards peak fitness.** Try not to offer solutions at this point; instead, give the player and parent time to agree some actions and come back with a very short list of their own.

5
Not every player who disengages is lazy.

I once encountered a player who had a habit of stopping immediately after giving the ball away to the opposition. If you read this you may be thinking...
"ONCE? I meet them all the time."

But this was different. It was as if someone had flicked a switch to OFF and the player could no longer move. He disengaged from the action completely, often with hands on hips and eyes to the sky; not for a second or two, but for as long as thirty seconds. To coaches and supporters it appeared as if he had taken a lazy fit and was unwilling to reset and work hard to help teammates win the ball back. After all, he was the player who had just lost it.

The problem didn't end after the initial period of inactivity. On nearly every occasion, he spent the next two or three minutes jogging, staying clear of any involvement and letting the game pass him by.

Any player, in any team, is going to give the ball away a number of times in a game. He's going to drop it, miss a lift, lose it in contact or misdirect a pass. Few are able to immediately dismiss their mistakes. Perhaps this is one of the traits that sets the best apart from the rest. Still, this particular player's reaction was extreme.

It took more than a few chats between our player and others to discover what lay behind the switching off. It turns out he was beating himself up for making the mistake. Nothing mattered other than reflecting on what had just happened. His thoughts didn't include anything about how to minimise the consequences of losing the ball and the possibility of winning it back again. They were entirely focussed on the loss. He wasn't lazy; he was consumed.

Talking it through seemed to help. The player benefitted by calling to mind his propensity for dwelling on mistakes. It may appear to be the complete opposite of what we think would help, but it did. Before he started each training game or competition game, he left it behind… in his kit bag… in the changing room.

What worked for him may not work for another player. Still, the different solutions are not the focus here. What's important to note is that there are players out there with the same habit; it's holding them back. Coaches can start by talking with them.

6
The player with a sideline parent/coach needs the club to step up

I'm not sure there are as many of these now as in years gone by. More and more players are coming from non-GAA backgrounds. Their parents may not even attend games, never mind join an ad hoc coaching chorus.
Yes, we've all heard the shouts from behind the wire, the parent directing the next play for a son or daughter. Some of the more common are:

'Go by him.'
'Take her on.'
'Back, back. Get back and help.'
'Who are you marking?'
'Where's your man?'
'Give it now…..NOW!'

The calls are often punctuated by enough periods of silence to make them bearable, but there are a few parents who are in there more often than a radio commentator. They don't do it to contradict the coach; they don't do it in anger; they just can't help it……or so they say.

It's a tough one to address, given that loud instruction (and plenty of it) has long been a part of our approach to coaching. Are parents simply copying phrases heard on the sideline?

One of the better ways to tackle the issue involves pre-game communication. In more than one club, coaches have used phone contact groups to coax parents down a different road. Here is an example of one those communications:

*"Good morning everyone; today we are asking for plenty of support for our players as they take part in the tournament. Please encourage the boys and give them a boost by doing so. We also ask all spectators to **avoid instructing players (particularly their own children) during games.** Coaches are currently working with the boys to help them....*

- *Develop their problem-solving skills.*
- *Improve their decision-making abilities.*
- *Become more creative on the pitch.*

Too much instruction can hinder their progress. Enjoy the day.

7
There are players who like to be challenged... ..and others who have yet to find out that they do too.

Think back to your childhood, when you had a day at the seaside. Whether or not you called them challenges, there was always an element of competition when there was water about. Who could skim pebbles and get most hops? Who could hit a distant rock with a stone? Who could jump the waves?
Players, young and not so, love challenges. Some prefer those that pit them directly against others. Some favour the more subtle approach, where they face a challenge that calls for thinking, action and even stealth.

Be prepared to experiment for different reasons. You'll want to find the appropriate level of challenge for different players and groups. Do you start with an easy task or do you set something tougher and give them time to work it out for themselves? Much of what's being promoted nowadays will push you towards the latter.

The idea is that you set a challenge and let the player(s) work out how best to meet it. In a team game, doing so may depend very much on the actions of others, so it makes sense to give players time before a game to discuss plans. An example:

Score from a run in behind the opposition defence.

The coach has set up a 9v9 training game (Reds v Greens) and has set the Red team this challenge. The team gets a few minutes to ask and answer their own questions.

What will we do to create space for this to happen?
Should we get our inside players to run out towards the ball?
Who might be the best players to make the run behind?
Where will they start their runs?
What type of pass is most likely to work?
Would a diagonal kick pass be better than a fist pass?

While the Reds discuss tactics, the Greens cannot simply be left to wait for them to finish. Why not set a different challenge for the Green team? Assign a coach to each team and have them watch to see how often teams meet their respective challenges. After the game, have a chat with both teams. Did any player spot what the opposition was trying to do?

You can help players and teams get used to being challenged by giving them more time to discuss and/or by giving them prompts. This comes under the umbrella of *scaffolding,* a way of providing temporary support for learners in order to help them to complete a task or acquire a skill, and then gradually withdrawing that support. Rather than being overwhelmed by a challenge, players are more motivated to face it.

8
Some players are serial complainers and may not know it.

I'm not talking here about the player who has a moment now and then and cannot hide his frustration as a good move is ruined or a goal comes as a result of poor marking. No...this is about the serial complainer, the chronic one who never seems to miss training or games and who is generally rated as one of the better players on the team.

If you don't have one of these, just skip forward to the next topic and don't weigh yourself down with worry about one of his ilk suddenly turning up to play. If you do have an energy vampire, then read on.

The first thing to consider is that the complainer may not even be aware that he is one. That may seem implausible but it's often true. A manager once talked to us about a player who appeared to fit this bill and explained his behaviour as being understandable because *"he comes from a long line of complainers."* At the time, his comment caused a fair bit of mirth but it did strike a chord. Maybe that's all he knows. Maybe that's the norm in the house.

So, your player may not know how discouraging and draining his words are, when he speaks. The flip side of that coin is the moaner who knows exactly what he's doing and to whom it is directed. More often than not, he will vent about mistakes made by those who belong to the following groups:

- Lesser skilled players
- Younger players
- Players not in his friendship group.

If someone ticks all three boxes, there's trouble coming.

Thankfully these troublemakers are few and far between and you are more likely to meet the former type of complainer. How might you make things better for the targeted players and for the person finding fault? The golden rule is never to react immediately and call out the wrongdoer. That can cause many more problems than it solves. Friends may side with him; you may embarrass the person being picked upon.

It's not easy. You may feel that fighting fire with fire will establish your position as boss, but it won't. If the player is on a youth or underage team, the situation can be made worse as parents become involved. Best to discuss it with other mentors first and find out their views on whether or not things need addressed and, if so, how to address them. Hoping that it will go away is not something to consider; not if you have already established that it is a recurrent theme.

I know of one sports club where it was highlighted at a pre-season meeting for youth players and parents under the title of *'The No Complaining Rule'*. You may be aghast at this move, but the detail should allay your fears. Players were asked to keep any complaints away from the pitch during training and during games. One member of the management team was designated as the *'Listener'* (I kid you not) and the news of his new role was delivered with plenty of humour.

Players were invited to speak with him immediately after training or a game, if they had anything to say. Everything on the pitch had to be positive, including attitudes to mistakes.
The net result? Nobody approached the listener. The rule and the post-holder are both still in place.

Not everyone would be capable of addressing the situation in such a novel fashion; many more will opt for the quiet approach and a discussion. That can work too. The offender gets to talk, the coaches get to listen and advise and the first step is taken. It may end with the adult saying... *"I'm going to give every player time to learn and I need you to do the same."*

9
There are those who learn best when given a choice.

Playing targets have always proved to be somewhat controversial. Advocates point to how they narrow the focus for a player and free him from other demands, while critics use the same verb *'narrow'* to talk of how targets will limit the player and deny freedoms.

It's a horses for courses topic for me and I've seen players respond positively to targets, while others just don't make much progress when they are set. Maybe it's more about the type of targets we set and how rigid we make them.

If we set targets for such things as scoring, fielding or tackling, they skew the game for the player and for others. Let's say a coach sets a target of 1-1 for a full forward during a training game. The player may end up trying to get on the ball when it's not the best idea and holding onto possession when a pass is the better option. Similarly with fielding kickouts and making tackles. They may draw the player into situations where he is not needed. For example...jumping against a teammate or rushing in to foul.

Last year I wrote about a model of coaching delivery which I named CAD. It is an attempt to get coaches to view what they do on the pitch in terms of..

- Command
- Assist
- Delegate

Command is driven by strict instruction.
Assist is about suggestions and flexibility.
Delegate means neither instruction or suggestion.

I would argue that setting targets based on the **assist** part of the model, is an ideal way to strike a balance between narrowing the focus and denying freedoms. So…instead of setting a 1-1 scoring target, the coach might ask the player to use the training game to practise choosing the better option between taking a shot and giving a pass.

The fielding target would be more about choosing when it's best to compete in the air, watch for the breaking ball or make a run to become an outlet for a pass. The tackling one can be an opportunity to focus on footwork (eg a narrower stance with feet moving rather than wide stance and fixed back on heels).

Setting targets with an element of saying to the player *'you choose when'* can hand over decisions and make for a better rapport between player and coach.

10
If you spot a player who finds it difficult to mix with teammates, find out more.

Learn to watch for it. Can you and other mentors distinguish between a player who is happy in his own company from someone who cannot fit in?
It's not an exact science, but there are signs. One of the better indicators happens before the coaching session begins. As players step onto the pitch, watch how they interact. Usually there's a kickabout.

Who gets involved straightaway?
Who is calling for and getting passes?
Who is taking shots at goal?
Who makes a beeline for a group and joins in the chat?
Who moves away to a bigger space and begins to kick a ball back and forth with another player?
Who doesn't do any of these things?
Yes, there's always the danger that you slip quickly into the world of confirmation bias and begin to see what isn't there. A word with fellow coaches and a commitment from all to keep an eye over the next few sessions will help. You're not looking for a blip. You're looking for a habit.

Let's jump forward to the point where the evidence suggests the player is finding it difficult to fit in. There may be many reasons for this and none may involve him being deliberately left out by others.

Lack of confidence in his own playing abilities is often a key element. Anonymity within the group is another. You can make the environment welcoming and safe for this player. You don't have to shield him from every single thing he may encounter during a training session, but you can ensure you're not adding to his woes.

Make sure you don't allow players to pick teams. That's just inviting an opportunity to embarrass him. There are lots of ways to sort teams and groups without having a 'best to worst' as part of your session.
That doesn't mean the player (and others) can't be split into proficiency groups for some parts of a session…eg a small-sided game….but have that thought out well in advance and make sure the coaching received by both groups is quality stuff.

Whether you believe it or not, you may be the constant in that player's sporting life. There may be nothing more protective for that young person than realising that you know his name.

So, call him by name when you are involving him. Praise him but don't deliberately steer clear of challenging him or correcting him. He can pick up when a coach only corrects the better-skilled players. He may be passing through a particularly vulnerable phase, but he is listening. Hearing his name means he matters. Ensure that other coaches know this too.

11
When you discover a player who is an innovator, have regular conversations.

An interesting one here, for we are inclined to believe there will be very few of this type of player. Yes…if we think about him as an orchestrator during games; the player who talks through the action, shows others the way, encourages, supports and dictates much of what happens throughout.

But are we confusing leadership with innovation? Leaders tend to stand up for coaches to see them early days, but innovators can be missed. A coach may never get to find out who has really good ideas if players aren't consulted and questioned.

Some of the best coaches already had innovative ideas in their heads while they were still players, but they were never asked for them. Not until they took on a role where ideas could be expressed, did others get to know how they thought. For a long time, our training sessions were not set up for players to share with coaches and managers.

Thankfully, in the past few years, conversations from peer to peer and between player and coach have become much more common. Coaches are more likely to set challenges for teams and have players discuss these before taking part in training games. When mentors listen in rather than give instructions or offer suggestions, they may learn who is an ideas person. Who thinks differently and can express those thoughts when given an opportunity?

I'm not suggesting that, by simply presenting players with challenges and being more inclusive, you will discover a hidden pool of innovators. It's unlikely. What you may do, is find one or two who add something new and who will help with both team and management learning.

I'll make one final point on this. If you create a number of player groups with established leaders in charge of each, you may be minimising the chances of finding those innovators. When the leader's voice is the only one being heard, there's no guarantee that others will put forward ideas.

No...this search for someone different has to be engineered. Put all the generals in one group and create the remaining groups from the infantry. The latter may be where you find your innovator.

12
Evasion often fails due to one tiny detail

The lesson here is about player actions that prevent him from executing a move, rather than physical attributes that hinder him. It's about the player in possession who has all the raw materials but can't seem to develop the product. What do I mean by this?

Think of the player who possesses the speed, power and agility to go past opponents when carrying the ball, but something doesn't quite click. One school of thought is that he will learn to adapt through participation only. He doesn't need a coach for prompts or triggers.

Supporters of this approach would argue that any help given wouldn't be contextual….that is, he'd be coached to learn an evasion move away from the game (eg 1v1 practice) but that wouldn't mean he could replicate it in the game. I do see merit in that argument, but I still favour intervention to offer a hint or two, rather than full discovery learning.

The reason I say this is that I've seen people change after being given a trigger. I've also seen them totally confused when given a list of instructions and I still hear that barrage of commands from some coaches. A list of possibilities in your head should not become a stream of instructions for a player. He just won't cope and neither would you if the roles were reversed.

The trick is to offer one suggestion at a time, but only after you have paid attention to what the player actually does in a number of training games and competition games too. If he repeats the same action in different situations, chances are it's his go-to method; it isn't working and he may not even be aware of it. Here are some examples of player habits that I've seen and that have, after time and effort on alternatives, been much reduced.

A player who strode positively with the ball in open play but changed to take much shorter steps as he approached a contact situation. He was as much as five metres away when it happened. Not only did he shorten his steps, he took lots of these in quick succession. Perhaps he believed that the speedy foot strikes would confuse an opponent; they didn't.
He saw clips on video, hadn't realised he was doing it and worked hard to maintain a longer stride throughout.

A player who had a feint and sidestep in his armoury, but rarely seemed to throw an opponent off balance and create the room to get past. More often than not, the tackler didn't buy the feint. The reason he wasn't having any success was because he only feinted with his leg. Instead of head, shoulder, arm and hip moving in tandem with that leg, they all leaned towards the opposite side, giving his plans away.

So, if the player wanted to pretend to go left in order to go right, most parts of his body were already moving right. He was easily caught. What worked for him was actually holding the ball in both hands and using it to start the move. Two-handed, he would reach the ball left. His whole body shifted left too and then he stepped to the right and away (again led by the ball).

A player who had learned a perfect shoulder roll, spinning 360° with ease. Trouble was, he often started his action far too early, well before any contact. This resulted in him still facing the tackler after having rolled at the wrong moment. Over time, he got the feel of it through association. He learned to think of himself as a door, hinged to a frame. When door and frame met, he rolled. It's still a work in progress.

One detail may be the breakthrough for a player. It's worth exploring and experimenting.

13
Peer mentoring can be more powerful than coach talk

Some coaches start a season by giving each player an opportunity to write a positive comment about everyone else on the squad. These are collated, typed up and presented. No sources are revealed. It sounds like a good idea and a confidence booster for many.

I'm reluctant to run this as an exercise for a full squad. Perhaps I'm concerned about players trying to find something meaningful to say about each teammate and struggling to do so for at least half of the squad.

If you are the CHB and your list comes back to you with references to... *'strength, confidence, aggression, control, awareness and leadership'*... you'll be happy. If, on the other hand, you usually get the number 23 jersey, will it help to read the words *dedicated club man*? I would argue that many players will interpret this comment as... *turns up regularly.*

How might we pass on the messages of support in a more meaningful way? One way is to establish a *peer mentoring programme.* Any mention of a programme may conjure up thoughts of action plans and targets. Forget that. In this case, it's just about connecting, encouraging and suggesting.
How does it work?

Within any squad will be one or two experienced and skilful players who are leaders and communicators. These are easily identified. What may be more difficult to pick out are those players who would benefit from an established team player having a role to play in their development, even for a brief period.

Let's be conservative here and say that you only identify one such player. That leaves two possible mentors for one mentee. One for one is probably the way to go, at least for a while. How to make it work?
Here's one method and an example to fit.

Paul was part of an U15 squad. He turned up week in week out for training, but rarely started a game.
His pitch play was best summed up by the word…**hesitant.** He got plenty of encouragement and direction from his coaches, but little changed.

A member of the management team had read about an initiative from basketball, linking peer with peer and driving development among players. The management team agreed that Cathal would be a good fit as a mentor and he agreed to take part.

Key parts of the plan were:

Coaches met with Cathal to agree the process, including the need to prioritise only **one** area and to deliberately look for opportunities to encourage and praise.

One coach met with Cathal and Paul to explain the basics of this particular approach…ie **both would play on the same team for most/all training games over the next month.**

What happened?

Paul's focus for the month of training games was to **move the ball on before contact.** At first, the thought was that a second focus could be added. Moving the ball before contact seemed like something that could be achieved quite quickly and with little difficulty. Wrong. Not only had Paul to learn when to pass the ball, he also had to pick out a receiver for the pass. Combining both was a challenge. His carrying habit had led to him rarely having to make decisions on both. It took the full month to get him motoring.

Cathal's input was excellent. Before every training game, he reminded Paul of his target. During the games he took opportunities to praise and after each session he spoke briefly with Paul about progress.

There may be some who think… *"all that effort just for one player and for only one part of his game."* That's understandable. But development takes time and it often has to be directed at one player. The benefit for Paul was that, not only did his possession game improve, but his self-esteem was raised too. He was important. He belonged.

14
Make sure you understand the true meaning of readiness

If you are a lead coach it's not enough to get yourself ready for a session. The very word **lead** means you have to think of others. Yes, the obvious others are the players and there is no doubt that many lead coaches put in a huge effort making sure that players get the most from training sessions.

But what about fellow coaches?
Not only will they appreciate knowing the content of the session beforehand, they also need that knowledge to prepare their own input, suggest an additional activity or even an alternative. They will play about with numbers, thinking of how an activity will run if 8 turn up or 15 or 20.

The fact that you do clue in your coaches can help with your session design. You will put more thought into it. You'll set out the different activities and, if you are open to change, you will invite responses. Of course, you don't have to accede to all requests but the sharing of information brings inclusion and a sense of belonging for all in the management team.

If you haven't been doing so, start now. You won't regret it.

15
Settle only for the appropriate equipment and plenty of it.

Unfortunately I've been to clubs where, not only is equipment lacking, but the quality of what's in use has been dire. You may feel I'm being harsh, but I would argue that there's no excuse for the wrong stuff, the lack of stuff and the poor maintenance of what's there. When clubs can afford to bring in a senior management team and still struggle to equip their nursery and youth teams, there's something wrong.

I'm not talking about huge sums of money here. The biggest cost will be playing equipment (eg footballs). That very expense would suggest that when you buy, you take care of them. Invest in an electric pump and always have spare valves to hand. Footballs deflate, almost as if they were doing so just to annoy you. Be ready and get them ready. A partly inflated football changes everything with a pass or a shot.

Bibs are another target area. Imagine you are running an U9 session and you're checking the club equipment store for some bibs. You find three of one colour, four of another, two ripped, others covered in dried mud and all of them big enough to make the U9s appear as if they are wearing dresses. Making do is not on. Investing in equipment means you are investing in players and coaches.

16
Getting coach:player ratios right is a major plus

A good way to measure coach:player ratios is to set the number of players who turn up on a good day against the number of coaches who turn up **regularly**. There's no point counting five coaches if only three make it to sessions on a regular basis. So….write down the true ratio and aim for the ideal one. There are lots of notions about what constitutes the ideal coach:player ratio with different age groups. Here are mine:

U6/Nursery   1:3   U8/U10   1:5
U12/U14/U16 1:7   Minor/Adult 1:8

Now…let's clarify who may be included. We must count parents (helpers/assistants) with the youngest group. Without them, a nursery session can quickly become a birthday party minus the bouncy castle. Few clubs would be able to make that 1:3 ratio using coaches alone. Some clubs have a rule…one parent or guardian must stay with the child throughout the session and be ready to help. A fellow club coach used to call these people his *accidental coaches.*

It's not easy getting that ratio to ideal levels but it's worth it. Being able to create different groups and teams and design an array of activities often begins with getting the ratio sorted. More about this when I get to my views on coaching roles.

17
Try not to rely on others for access to facilities

Something that you may feel doesn't belong in a coaching book but I can assure you, it's crucial. Forget about the link to session preparation and think safety instead.

If the gates are locked, parents and players may be queuing in traffic. My own club is on a main road. Even with a filter lane, it can present a problem. That's why the gates are open from early morning until late.

Now to the session itself. Not having easy access to equipment can throw plans into disarray. Somebody has promised to be there, but has been held up. Ten minutes turn into twenty and thirty.

Argue your case for a set of keys or have the club use combination locks. It may not be long until entry is via electronic pass; some clubs already have it. Whatever way you decide to sort it, don't delay.

18
Coaching bilateral skills can be a long litany of dietary lapses.

There's plenty of alliteration in that title and it serves as a reminder to us that committing to work on left and right sides (feet and hands) is one thing; persevering with it is another. Hence the reference to lapses and diet.

We all know the value of being able to use right and left comfortably while playing the game. We coaches start with the best of intentions and, as players stumble through the early and middle days of learning, our dream of turning out a youth team with several players being able to pass and score off both sides, can disappear over the horizon.

To add weight to our excuses, we remind ourselves that there are very few players, even at senior county level, who can switch hand or foot when needed, passing and scoring and having us wonder which side really is the stronger. Surely these players are just born special and home grown thereafter. No amount of coaching will ever deliver the bilateral dream team; and that part is true.

What we can do is light the fire in players to practise. Our weekly or twice weekly sessions can help in that regard, but the huge bulk of work must be done away from the training ground. Add to that, the desire a player must have to truly become bilateral and you can see the challenge isn't an easy one. Still, there are things we can do to help. Here are a few:

Devise a skills test which focuses on bilateral skills. Make sure it has passing and scoring included.

Alert coaches to things that tend to put players off working on both sides.

- ➢ A major one for fist passing is throwing the ball into the air before striking it. The pass from this throw rarely looks good.
- ➢ Kicking from the hands also presents a problem. Many will stand 'stork-like' in one spot, while trying to throw a leg out at the ball as it drops. Starting the kicking action with a step forward makes it much easier for the player.

Highlight players from county teams who are two-sided. *"Let's work on our Clifford and Walsh skills."* sounds much more inviting than *"Let's work on our weak side."*

19
Changes of pace are serious weapons
we may not use enough.

It's not the case that we don't know they exist and it's rarely that we don't recognise them when we see them happen on the pitch. My own view is that we have them way down our list of coaching needs; perhaps they don't even make the list. So…let's see if I can make a case for pushing them up that list.

If we want players to practise different ways to make room for passes and shots, we must at least remind them to experiment with changes of pace. I've phrased it this way because there are players who already use them regularly and there are those who will learn them after a reminder and without intervention. There's also another group, made up of players who will benefit from some coaching.

The coach doesn't have to be an expert on running mechanics, for the problem may be that a player is simply mistiming when to change pace. One of the bigger obstacles to successfully evading an opponent is that the ball carrier doesn't change pace after making room and can't get away.

Still, if it does turn out to be a question of poor technique, then someone to help with running mechanics would be the next port of call.

20
Drills and Games – look for an ideal balance

It seems that for years and years we all missed a trick by not playing enough games in our training sessions. I know that my typical session would have had a warm-up, followed by three or four favourite drills and a game to finish. Time management wasn't a strength, so the game at the end often suffered. Twenty promised minutes quickly turned into ten or fewer.
As far as I was concerned, most of the learning had taken place during the drills. Not so!

Not until my good friend Terence McWilliams introduced me to the 'Whole-Part-Whole' concept, did I begin to see more worth in games. More of my sessions started with games, broke for relevant practice of one or two game elements (eg tackling and shooting) and then returned to the game for more practice. Gameplay was now getting a bigger slice of the session cake.

Nowadays, the science behind how players learn is convincing us to use different game types, game sizes and game structures to promote learning. We may think we will miss the drills, but contextual learning is better. Explore this topic as often as you can and keep abreast of new developments across different team sports. Go find new ways.

21
Coaching isn't as much about variety nowadays

I once heard a senior footballer extol the virtues of a coach by saying *"In a whole season, he never did the same drill twice."*

Before you to talk back to the page and berate the coach for running drills rather than games, I must tell you this was more than a decade ago. Activity aside, the player appeared to value the non-repetition quite highly.

Fair play to that coach. To have amassed a portfolio of training exercises demanded dedication, research and no small measure of invention. I knew the man well and for him it was never about a new drill every time; it was about tweaking things to keep people motivated.

His experience had told him that players can be lacklustre in their approach when presented with the same menu of drills, week upon week.

Nowadays, there appears to be much less of an emphasis on providing variety of that sort. Have players bought more into repetition? I suspect not. For me it's really about the shift from drill-based to game-based coaching.

As coaches embrace the practice of developing players and teams via a game-based approach, there are fewer spaces to fit in drills. If a session is filled with games, the basic ingredients are different sizes of playing area and different sizes of teams.

Into the mix can go some constraints, but the mechanics of who goes where, how many players at each cone, who passes to who and how many footballs are needed, no longer apply.

When you think about it, many of us spent years devising drills where we devoted more time and energy to working out how to ensure all the moving parts were slick and well-oiled, than we did to thinking about the worth of the exercises themselves.

Coaching through games is an altogether easier method when it comes to planning, though it demands different observation skills when it's happening.

22
Coached attacking play does not deny players opportunities to be creative

I have long held a belief that the *'denying creativity'* argument is often put forward by those who find attacking play difficult to coach…..and it can be.

Rather than search for answers and filter out those that work on paper but not on the pitch, they choose to place attacking play in the *'Player Imagination'* box and close the lid.

They may even go as far as describing coached attacking as..

1 passes to 2
2 passes to 3
3 gives it to 4
4 shoots.
Repeat, repeat.

This gives the impression of coaching that is formulaic and, as such, robotic. Nothing could be further from the truth.

There is no doubt that creativity and imagination have roles to play, but not to the exclusion of everything else. There are players who see things others do not, who can pick out passes which demand precision and timing that does not come easily to many. Are we forgetting that players can learn to be creative? The verb *'create'* brings with it so many applications within the game. Players might learn to…

- *Create space for others use*
- *Create scoring opportunities*
- *Create width and depth*
- *Create distractions*

So, when a coach sets out three channels in the attacking half of the pitch, he/she is really inviting players to be creative.

Some will have ideas of their own, some will need prompts, some will buy into instruction. That's just one example of coached attacking and it certainly does not deny opportunities to be creative.

23
Defensive coaching can be confusing

In an earlier part of this book I wrote…

When the opposition has the ball, decision-making may actually be a little easier, because so many coaches are giving players set defending positions and specific roles in those positions.

"If we lose the ball, drop back inside the 45."
"Get back immediately to protect the D."
"If you're in a wide position, tuck in to this part of the pitch. No point staying wide. They won't score from out there."
"If you lose the ball, your job is to chase it to win it back. Don't worry about covering. Others will be doing that."

I stand by that assertion, but only in terms of player decision-making. However, I have found it an altogether different proposition trying to coach players what to do when they get into those positions.

Who tackles?
Who hands over an opponent to a teammate?
When should that handover happen?
What is a drift defence?
How will I coach communication between players?

I have watched coaches at club and county level devise and deliver lots of ideas on defending. On many occasions, players have responded positively and built a more solid defence as a result.

Still, having watched good people at work, I have moved no further forward with my defensive coaching skills. So, if you were hoping for some enlightenment here, the best I can offer is...if you need help on how to set up and operate a defence, find a coach who has had success doing so and whose communication skills will inspire both players and other coaches.

Players may also prove to be very helpful in this regard, particularly with older groups eg. minor and adult.
If you hand over responsibility to players and allow them to experiment with a variety of defensive set ups, the least you will get will be engagement and the best outcome will be a couple of answers and ownership.

24
Sooner or later I was bound to focus on coaching the individual (PDC)

Why am I giving over a bitesize lesson to PDC (Player Development Coaching)? There's a simple answer. I find that many coaches are either content to have a passing acquaintance with PDC or they find lots of excuses for not pursuing it at all. We need more coaches paying more attention to individuals.

Chief among reasons not to adopt PDC as a core part of coaching is the age-old... *"We find it tough enough to get people to take a team, never mind get people to coach individual players."*

I get it. The original idea was for a squad to have a dedicated coach working with individuals to improve technical skills. The example I often used was where a player (or two players) might step away from the squad training for 10 minutes to work on tackling or scoring or fielding. They would then return to the collective training and be replaced by two others. This format would be repeated for as long as it took to effect some change. It had the appearance of a sustained coaching clinic.

For this to work, a number of things had to be put in place. These included:

> Having a coach willing to do this work
> Having a coach able to do this work
> Starting the process with top players, in order to remove any stigma that might be associated (e.g. PDC is only for those not making the team).
> Making sure the skills gaps were genuine and not a case of us making work for ourselves.

Coaches prepared to take on such a role are few and far between. This doesn't mean they don't exist, but it does highlight that lots of coaches may not be comfortable working in isolation and on the specifics of technical skills. They much prefer to stay with the group. The newer approach to PDC allows coaches to stay together with the group and still be focussed on specifics. The emphasis has shifted away from helping improve technical skills to assisting players as they strive to develop better decision-making skills in the game.

This seems to appeal to more coaches. Is it because they can perform the role while enjoying the safety of the pack? Is it because they feel they've been doing it for ages and PDC is just a new label? Whatever the case, the switch from out-of-game coaching to an in-game focus has definitely whetted more appetites.

Let's hope the day isn't far away when the majority of coaches and players are agreeing priority challenges and working together to find a way.

25
Creating teamplayers isn't as difficult as it used to be.

In years gone by, our typical training session would have seen an 80/20 (even a 90/10) split in favour of drills over games. Many of those drills would have been unopposed, though the push to get quicker was always there. Solo running was also a thing. Long carries were fairly common and weren't just attempted by the accomplished practitioners. We all had a go.
The game at the end….and it was always that…was often our only opportunity to work together in combinations greater than two. Not surprisingly, these opportunities were not taken as often nor as well as they might have been. How could they? There had been no rehearsal for this; no building up to the bigger game.

What transpired was a long ball game of kick and catch and drop and fight for the break. Some people cry out for its return, though I suspect most did not play in that era and, if they did, they only remember the good games like they do good summers.

The increasing practice of game-based coaching and the exposure to teamplay that it affords, has led to more and more players getting comfortable with all types of passing and movement and recognising the value of interplay. Long may it continue. Teamplayers are here to stay.

26
Position rotation is a great way for players to learn.

The learning from this practice comes in many forms. Some may learn to favour a particular position that they had never played before; others may find out how difficult it is to play in a certain position and come to appreciate those who line out there regularly.

Much of the position rotation happens when players are still in the 'Go Games' phase. The small-sided approach makes it quite easy to swap players between goals, backs, midfield and forwards across four or five tournament games.

A coach at my own club once described the rotation as *"Like eating different vegetables…you may like some more than others, but they're all good for you."* His announcement wasn't cheered from the rooftops, but he was correct. Playing in different positions is good for learning.

There are numerous examples of players who began as forwards, struggled with some of the demands and found that a half-back role suited them better. It could be down to something as simple as facing the play rather than winning the ball and turning.

27
TACOS is an easy way to plan kickouts and give everyone a role.

It's an easy acronym to remember, whether you are a coach or a player. All it does is detail some things you may want to think about when designing kickouts, particularly those that are hit long.

T = Target
Where do you want the ball to land? Who do you want to target as the receiver? How do you intend to make it easier for the receiver to win the ball?

A = Assist
Which teammates will support the targeted player, either to win any breaking ball or to take a pass from the ball winner?

C = Cover
Which players will ignore the urge to assist at the point where the ball lands and, instead, move to shore up the defence? Their job is to be ready in case the opponents steal the ball from your kickout.

O = Open
How will you open up the opposition defence to allow the attack to develop after winning the ball from the kickout? Who will move for a pass? Who will run decoy?

S = Start
How will your kickout begin....with a signal or a call? Will players set up in a certain formation to enable a particular kickout?

Play about with TACOS. Use a tactics board and move your numbered players about to see what looks good as a simulation. Run it unopposed on the pitch and with everyone involved. Perfect it with passive opposition.

Eg.

T   12 runs from the far 45m to receive on the wing.
A   7, 8 and 6 make support runs at pace.
C   9, 10 and 5 cover behind the ball with 2, 3 and 4.
O   15, 14, 11 and 13 all run wide to open the middle.
S   1 starts the kickout with a signal for all to bunch.

28
Getting to know players is not a bonus...it's a must.

I may have mentioned this story in another book, but it's relevant here and worth retelling.

There was once a consultant who worked in a maternity unit of a large hospital. He had been there for years and had got to know lots of mothers and they him. When mothers came in for the second, third or fourth time, he would often meet them on his rounds. Each time, he asked about their other children, always remembering names and appearing to correctly guess ages. These were all conversation starters to put people at ease while carrying out medical checks.

What few knew was that, in his notes, he had previously recorded names, dates of birth and other bits and pieces of family information and was able to refer to these without appearing to look them up.
Nobody expected him to be able to call to mind the details that he did, but all saw the value in his methods.

Coaches can do the same, when getting to know players. There are only a handful who can retain information in their heads about players, other than that which relates to training and playing. If it helps to jot down a snippet or two to engage a player or help with a conversation, then do it.

If this practice has a hollow ring to it, that cannot be helped. It's no different to the advice given by so many others in the coaching world who write *"You have to show players that you care"* or *"players are people first and players second"*.

These are laudable aims but who can claim to properly know and remember details about all of the players in a squad without committing some information to paper?

If I was a player and my coach asked about my exam results and was able to name the three subjects, I'm pretty sure I would know he had written that information down, but I would still be impressed that he had taken time to do so and was asking at all.

These are the snippets that start conversations and open the door for chats about playing skills, habits, concerns and ambitions. They, in turn, will lead to player and coach getting to know more about each other and developing trust.

29
Team selection is a minefield, but doesn't have to be.

"We are agreed on 12 positions and the players to fill these. The other 3 are still up for grabs."

The manager who regularly spoke those words (with only the numbers changing from game to game) admitted years later that he and he alone picked the team.

There was never a management meeting or discussion. He wrote the team on a sheet of paper, handed it to his two selectors and invited them to circle any players from the list of substitutes, whom they felt deserved a starting place.

If they circled two players, his announcement to the squad was that they had agreed on thirteen, with two places still available. The manager would then quietly ask the selectors to make a case for the two substitutes, who they would replace and why.

Very often, the team stayed as he had written it, with the two quietly nominated as first subs. He then used the selectors' concerns to have a word with those who had survived the cut.

"We want to you get ahead of the ball more often in this game."
"Let's see lots of passing before contact during the first half."

I'm not saying that I agree with his thinking but I do acknowledge that he had a plan and he stuck to it. Many of us don't have a plan for team selection. We do have our 6 from 9 or our 12 from 15 in our heads, but often don't have any system in place for the remaining slots.

Speaking of a system that is thankfully on the wane, fewer of us are now allowing players to pick teams for training games. Maybe the shift towards game-based coaching has led to a realisation that taking time to sort teams for different games in advance of the session, is a worthwhile exercise. It helps with transition times between different activities.

More importantly, it means we get to think about match-ups, constraints we want to apply and combinations we want to see on the pitch. Yes, absenteeism and injury will always throw a spanner in the works, but these hiccups are not a reason to give up on sorting teams beforehand.

30
One of the best things you can do is assign coaching roles to selectors and mentors.

I wonder how many lead coaches are reluctant to do this because they cannot imagine someone else doing exactly as they ask. They see the need for others to work alongside them, but hold on tightly to the session reins and allocate menial tasks only.

One reason for not sharing the coaching load is mentor reluctance to step forward. A lead coach may interpret this as the person being happy with his/her current responsibilities and having no desire to coach.

Another reason can be perception of abilities. For some lead coaches, having others set up and run scenarios, drills or SSGs at the other end of the pitch is more worrying than comforting.

What are they telling players? How has she explained that activity? Why is he still talking? Is the intensity high enough?

Just as player learning may be scaffolded, so can coach learning. How long would it take to list two things for the coach to emphasise while running an exercise?

1. Ask players to practise using their four steps before bouncing or toe-tapping the ball.
2. Ask players to practise making solid contact on the ball when shooting.

Giving other coaches specific instructions can be energising for them. What's important is to ensure that the messages are clear, concise and limited to two maximum. How a message is conveyed is paramount. A positive message generates an emotional response and is more readily accepted. Check for understanding from the coaches and ask them to do likewise with players.

Once again, game-based coaching comes to the rescue when assigning meaningful roles to coaches. Run a training game; have your constraints or links or match-ups set. Referee that game and have coaches watch for specifics as the game unfolds.

Coach A: *Watch what Sean does when his team loses possession. Is he getting behind the ball?*

Coach B: *Keep an eye on how the blue team players attack. Are they still getting their spacing right?*

Dividing observation tasks among those on the sideline (even among injured players) is an excellent use of expertise and is so much better than simply asking people to watch the game. Feedback becomes more relevant and management teams gel as a result.

31
We all have a default coaching method and it's tough to let go.

It may not be recognisable under this title, but I like to call the method favoured for decades by the vast majority of coaches, **the command style.** It was handed down to us by our coaching forefathers and we kept it alive by continuing to instruct the next generation on how the game must be played. No questions, no discussion, just instruction. Tell them what to do and that's it.

Ok...so I'm laying it on a bit thick. Truth be told, it wasn't as bad as it sounds. Players were not railroaded into performing in ways that were alien to them; nor were they crying out for a greater say in game plans and tactics. Why? Because it was the norm to be coached by command and there was nothing else on the menu.

I'm taking a giant leap here, but I'm going to link the command coaching method with the equally strict methods of teaching and learning that happened in schools for generations.

Many coaches were teachers. As a teacher's daily work was founded on organising and educating by command, it made many of them favourites to be appointed managers and coaches. A school class became a squad and a classroom a pitch.

As teaching moved slowly away from the 'listen and follow' approach towards a blend of command, discussion and delegation in the classroom, so coaching has followed….or is trying to follow.

And that's where we are at this moment. Don't expect the year 2023 to see a huge upsurge in coaching that relegates the command style to second or third place behind the **assist** or **delegate** types. It was never a case of hoping it would; it was more about diluting its use and the latter two methods gaining some traction in club youth and underage programmes.

'**Assist'** coaching is all about offering choice rather than strict instruction. Feedback from players is welcomed and any adjustments are agreed between coach and players. An example may help you make sense of this explanation.

Rather than tell a player to stop carrying the ball into contact, the coach would allow the player to try and break through contact a maximum of twice during a 10-minute game. The player chooses when is best. The player also knows that a coach will observe and be on hand to discuss progress after the game. Together they decide what way to approach the next training game.

I have learned that there are lots of good coaches out there who find it difficult to adopt this approach. For many, it's the thought of devoting so much time and energy to one player that puts them off. It will take a while before coaches move readily in this direction. It may even take media reports of counties successfully implementing it, to convince club coaches of its worth.

The **delegate** style is often more appealing than **assist**. Teams are picked and let play. During breaks, players take charge of discussions with their respective teams and agree adjustments (if any). A coach may observe the discussions but not influence them.

Is it a risk to allow players to take charge of their own approach to a training game? Only if you expect it to run smoothly and for players to think as you do. I've found that, like many other learning opportunities, it needs time and space to get to the point where coaches and players are working in concert.

We all agree that learning is messy; but we find it more difficult to accept that phrase when it looms large in front of us.

32
It makes sense for coaches to learn sideline roles and responses.

No, it's not the wrong phrase. I didn't mean to write roles and responsibilities. It's definitely a lesson about responses. Think about the prep we do ahead of training sessions. There's no need to list things here and miss one or two. It's enough to say that the 'to do' jobs are numerous.

We often divide them up between us and know exactly what's required. Not so the prep for being on the sideline on game days.

Let's say we have a management team of three.
Who does what?
Has each of us got a role while the game is on?
Do we all stand close together or do we split?
Should we all have notebooks and pens?
Are we looking for specifics or not?
What stops us from commenting on every single mistake?
When do we report a concern?
Do we coach players during the game?
Are we influenced by what supporters shout?

Together, have we considered these questions and answered them?
Better still....**have we practised?**

Do we know how we will respond to different things the game might throw up?
Better still….**have we practised?**

What if one of our players is sent off?
What if we have an extra player?
What if the opposition changes to play a long ball game?
What if the change is to a running game?
What if our go-to forward is being well marked?
What way do we respond to an opposition sweeper?
Will we respond to each of these as we see fit on the day or should we practise our responses in training games and challenge matches?

We want players to be prepared for as many game situations as possible. What we also need to think about is getting our own management team ready for its sideline response.

For me, it's a no brainer….*take every opportunity in training to practise what you will have to do in competition games.*

33
Team talks are best left to a skilled orator

If you are lucky enough to have such a person on your management team, make sure he/she knows that there will be one pre-match team talk only and that any invitation for others to add to that talk will be politely declined. In other words, one person delivers.

Just think of a situation where players are about to leave the changing room after a clear, concise and motivating talk and another coach says....

"One more thing before you go....we've always lost to this lot and it stops today. No goals. No frees in the scoring zone either. No giving away a penalty like last time."

What an exit that would be!

What should be encouraged, of course, is plenty of involvement in the lead up to the talk. Make discussion part of the process. Offer ideas; listen to other coaches and players; compromise. Then, once there is agreement, let the orator loose.

The same applies to a halftime talk. There may be even more reason for one voice, as emotions may be running high and the last thing needed is a chorus of disjointed messages. Discuss away from the players; agree what will be said and say it.

What if there is no such person in your group? Might it be an idea for someone to set about learning how to give a good team talk?
Your first reaction to that question may be another question.
Who has time for that?
The answer is...
Anyone who sees a team talk as a valuable part of match day.

A straightforward internet search, using a phrase such as....*how to structure a team talk*....or......*how to improve a pre-match team talk*....will bring hundreds of results. It may take a while to find a template that catches your eye, but it will be worth it.

So...don't wing it, work at it.

34
Feedback can be an acquired taste.

For many coaches it's all about source. If the feedback is from players to coaches, then it may be something that is not immediately liked or appreciated.

The idea of players commenting on tactics in games or the merit of different activities in training can make some coaches feel that their efforts are being unfairly judged. The same coaches may be more comfortable giving feedback rather than receiving it.

"Players are children. They don't always know what's good for them. If we ask for feedback, they'll want the football equivalent of ice cream."

That statement came from someone who'd had lots of competition success, both as a player and as a mentor. Imagine a coach deliberating over the worth of player feedback and having to choose between what he has read on the subject and what this mentor has pronounced. There's a good chance he'll go local.

Still, the number of naysayers is dwindling. Soon the practice will be part of the fabric in clubs right across the country. There's nothing to fear about it, other than the unknown.

Only once did I get to the stage with a team where I could elicit feedback by simply saying…*"Ok, talk to me."* All others required layers of scaffolding to make conversations more meaningful. Sometimes it didn't work at all.

Feedback must not be allowed to morph into a regular moaning session. A coach may have to use a mix of questions, prompts and cues to focus attention in training games.

For example:

Coach: *So..we've been trying to open up that area in front of goal for passes. How do you think that went?*

Player A: *Well, none of us stood in there, that I saw. But they had a sweeper.*

Player B: *The sweeper was putting us off making runs through it; too much chance of a pass being cut out.*

Coach: *The sweeper is working for them. They won't move him. How do we counter that?*

No response from players.

Coach: *What about using that area in a different way? Let players occupy it, but keep the ball out of it.*

Player A: *But we won't be opening up the scoring zone then.*

Player C: *We're not opening it now. It's a training game. Why not? If it works, great. If it doesn't, we can come up with something else.*

This is proper feedback and discussion to try and solve a problem. Something that can also help promote even more player discussion is for the coach to pose the question and then step away for a minute or two.

With no member of the management team looking on, some players may express their thoughts more freely. The coach can return to hear ideas and agree what to try.

35
'In game' changes mean different things to different people.

Have you a plan or system in place for deciding on changes during games? Do you rotate players based on playing time? Do you feel that all players get ample playing time in challenge games? Are players aware of how you decide changes?

If you are coaching adults, you are unlikely to rotate players in and out of the game, based on time on the pitch. If you are in charge of an U13 team, you will be much more aware of the need for players to get ample game time and not just be labelled and used as substitutes.

Let's leave the adult game and focus on those early teenage squads. There's a lot of talk out there about proper game time, minimum 50% participation and meaningful involvement for all, but there's not a lot of action.

Most administrations, when setting up leagues and championships and determining game structures, are not prioritising the 50%+ rule. They are providing a programme of fixtures that ensures all clubs get equal playing time but not all players.

You might ask...how could they ever hope to ensure a more even spread of playing time for individuals? That's a job for clubs, managers and coaches. But it's too easy to accept that argument. The administrators can help. They can offer a game template that facilitates fair playing time for all in their early teenage years.

The advent of Go Games brought about equal playing time for all, based on there being no substitutes. I'm sure some of you reading this will be fit to point to examples of clubs breaking that rule and you may even excuse it. But for most clubs across the country, it was a rule worth keeping and playing by.

So...a squad of 20 players starts with a club, all 5 years of age. Those 20 players get to play every minute until they reach 12 years of age. As U13s, 7 of the 20 will now start each game on the bench; and the authorities wonder why player retention is a problem?

A couple of years ago, a four-quarter template was suggested. It showed how all players on a squad could get 50%+ playing time in each game. If two squads of different sizes turned up for a game, there was a ready reckoner available to help. The four-quarter model was rejected. It was good enough and workable enough as a way to build in water breaks during the pandemic; why not as a way to guarantee participation and hope to retain a greater percentage of teenage players ?

Some objected to its introduction because they were traditional two-half people. Some said, without trialling it, that the changeovers after every 15 minutes would be cumbersome and break the momentum of the game. Some claimed it would lead to the better players leaving for other sports….this as a result of them finding out their time on the pitch would be reduced.

Had they forgotten that many of the more skilled players were also getting game time with school teams and development squads? Club U13 substitutes do not get those opportunities. They only have one avenue open to them.

The same people have yet to offer viable alternatives; but then again, if they are administrators, perhaps it's not their job. It's down to coaches, parents and other educators to convince them.

36
The most successful coach recruiters do house calls.

Earlier in the book I mentioned a coach in my own club, who recruited his coaches from a cohort of unsuspecting parents as they sat in their cars. The knock on the window was followed by a simple request:

"Is there a chance you could give me a hand for a few minutes?"

Anyone who stepped out of a vehicle was hooked. Most never got to sit in their cars, drink coffee and read the Sunday papers from that day forward. Marty D called them his *accidental coaches*. There are few of his ilk in clubs and that's what makes them special.

Still, for all the help that can be found to assist with coaching 5-11 age groups, the same cannot be said for the 12-19 groups. Lots of clubs struggle to recruit adults who are prepared to give some time to working with teenagers.

There are many reasons for this; they range from lack of confidence to an unwillingness to subject themselves to the rigour of background checks. One of the bigger stumbling blocks is simply a lack of awareness of how to help. That's why a home visit can be the difference between a missed opportunity and a fully signed up mentor.

The sales pitch (and that's what it is) needs to be clear, concise and well rehearsed. Just like the team talk, it is best delivered by a skilled club rep. Another key message is specificity.

You may not get far with a message that says *"Can you give a hand with the U14s this year?"* For many, that translates as two midweek evenings and a weekend morning from February to September. There's nothing in that message that sells. This one has a better chance of landing.

"I'd really like you to see these players. They would benefit so much from some advice on attacking.
If you could give us just one hour a week. You won't be running drills or picking teams or sorting equipment. You'll be watching them in training games and suggesting wee tweaks here and there that might help some of them improve their game."

Reduce the task to manageable levels, cut the time commitment and draw on that person's area of expertise (eg a former forward) to make the role sound enticing.

37
Parental contact is all about updating and educating.

Most clubs use different social media platforms to establish parental contact groups. The main reason is to stay in touch with young players and, in doing so, inform parents of dates, times and details of training sessions and games.

Having that direct link with parents also affords opportunities to educate. It's really about being able to clue parents in to how the club is working to help their children develop as players and as people. Parents get to learn via a season-long drip feed rather than by simply attending a single information evening. A combination of both is even better.

Here are a few examples of messages I've read:

U9s
The players are currently learning to fist pass accurately with right and left hands. Take a few minutes at home to find out how we use 'Head, Hands, Feet'. Find some time to practise with your son/daughter.

U15s
The squad will be working on new kickout moves next week. To help them learn, our goalkeepers really need everyone to attend both training sessions.

U6s
On Sunday we will be using our big square again. This is where the coaches will show parents and players how to practise the following:

- *Bouncing and catching when walking/running*
- *Running towards a ball to catch it*
- *Kicking a ball from the hand.*

The small squares are for parents and players to practise each of these skills. We will also have our usual relays, obstacle races and other fun events.

Keep in touch regularly and positively. Communication between coach and parent is important.

38
What players hear from coaches must be clear, encouraging and agreed.

How do you and your fellow coaches communicate with players during training and competition?
Are there lots of conflicting voices?
Do you agree on who speaks and when?
Is there a shouting match when someone wants to make a point?
Have you decided, as a group, to maintain an air of calmness in training and on the line?
Do you bring each other into line if things get loud?

If you read these six questions quickly, one after the other, it may suggest an uncontrolled and purposeless environment, with coaches vying for attention and players trying to make sense of it all. Rarely, if ever, is that the case. I certainly have not witnessed such a scene.

What I have witnessed, is a well-meaning cacophony of instruction…..an excess of information coming at players. I've not yet checked with any players to find out what sticks. Perhaps I should. I would need permission from coaches and I would have to be honest about my purpose.

Maybe it would sound more palatable if I told a body of coaches that I was keen to find out how well players concentrated when they were giving advice and issuing reminders. As long as the onus was on players, I think coaches would allow it.

But in many situations, the onus is not on players; it's on those delivering rather than on those receiving. For me, the most pervasive habit is *sending out conflicting messages.*

This tends to happen during play, when coaches are spread out around the pitch perimeter and often with an additional task to carry out. League games have one neutral official, the referee. Sideline officials and umpires are drawn from the two teams. If your management group has been split up to perform one or more of these duties, cohesion is often lost.

Coaches can begin to give instructions that were never agreed. Umpires, with more time and less movement than sideline officials, are more likely to offer advice.

A selection of umpire messages to those within earshot:

- *Make a run…show yourself early and let her see you.*
- *Somebody get in here. We've lost our shape.*
- *Go out the pitch and get yourself into the game.*
- *Mark him from the front.*
- *Let her go. She's no danger out there.*
- *Stay between him and the goal at all times.*

If these messages are in keeping with what has been agreed by management and players, they will help reinforce actions. If not, they can lead to indecision among players and disagreements among coaches.

> ➢ Let's say the team has been working on a running game, freeing up the D and the area inside the 20m line. How does *'Somebody get in here'* fit the template?

> ➢ Consider a situation where a forward has been working on holding her position for longer and leaving space for others. Then she hears a voice telling her to *make a run…show yourself early.*

There's still a distance to go in the quest for better messaging. All it needs is for management to agree what's useful and what's not and stick to it.

39
Communication between different age groups is largely absent.

Only in the past couple of years have I heard the phrase *'working in silos'* applied to coaching. This describes a situation when individuals and teams are working towards the same goal but they don't share or communicate enough. In a club where coaches work separately and without coordinating, a silo approach operates.

This doesn't necessarily mean that the work being done with different squads is sub-standard as a direct result. What I am suggesting is that a proper system of sharing will definitely lead to more discussion, more questions and more answers. Ideas and practices that may have been missed in *'silo coaching'* are set in front of everyone. People get to choose from a more varied menu.

During my school career, I was always fascinated by the fact that two teachers could work for years in rooms not ten feet apart, and never properly share ideas, tricks and tips. There were official CPD opportunities, but they tended to be generic and rarely aimed at individual classroom practice. Yes, personality was also a factor; what one person can carry off in a classroom can be very different to what another can. But these can all be used as excuses to not try something different.

If learning is messy for students, it can be messy for teachers too. The messiness is not an indicator that it isn't working.

So it is with players and coaches. If we expect players to learn, we should expect coaches to learn as well. All types of learning involve some change. If the change is to open the doors of the coaching silos and share, then it must be done.

Last year, during one workshop, I asked coaches to observe a friend of mine as he took charge of a 20-minute session with an U12 group. Afterwards, I asked for feedback.

"He let them play for longer than I would."
"When he calls them in, they run to him and then he only talks for about 30 seconds. Then they go again."
"I like the way he asks them to repeat what he has just told them."
"When he blows the whistle and puts his hand in the air, that's the signal to come in for more information."
"I haven't seen that game before. Have you a copy of how it works?"
"The big whiteboard is a great idea."
"He already had them bibbed during the warm-up."

In those seven comments, only one was about an activity. The others focussed on the coach's actions. Set up a forum for sharing. It may change how you coach.

40
Handovers can be perfect springboards for further development.

The season is over. Your squad is made up of a mix of U12 and U13 players. The latter group will leave to begin a new chapter, playing as the younger U15s next year. You are staying to coach next season's U13s. That's the scene set. Now let's think about handovers. The leavers' group has 14 players, each one with his/her own traits, habits, strengths and challenges. It's worth getting the management team together to reflect on how the season panned out for these players.

There are so many ways to collate information about each player and pass it on to the next management team. The temptation may be to include lots.
Why?
Any group discussion will generate loads of comments about a player. You may also feel you want to cover all bases. I'm not so sure about this approach. A long list can be off-putting, even if it's a mix of positives and challenges. Better to start with some brainstorming, build that list and then set about editing to make it more manageable and useful.

One way to edit is to use the '**Two Stars and a Wish**' template. This involves choosing two observations about a player's qualities (= the two stars) and making one suggestion for improvement (= the wish).

Here are some examples;

Player:	JB
Two Stars:	Lots of pace
	Strong tackler
A Wish:	Better first touch in possession
Player:	RT
Two Stars:	Scorer
	Two-sided
A Wish:	Improve work rate when possession is lost
Player:	PO'K
Two Stars:	Good fielder of a high ball
	Powerful solo runner
A Wish:	Play more 'pass and move' football

Handing over these summaries to the U15 coaches doesn't guarantee that they will use the information, especially if the practice isn't commonplace in the club.

In my experience, few clubs include it in reviews. There's more of a clean slate approach to the next season. Stars and wishes don't threaten that. They inform coaches.

41
S&C has its place...and that place is right at the heart of player development.

A few years ago I would never have imagined writing that sentence. For me, there was far too much emphasis on S&C. The easy way to damn it was to regularly refer to it as the fad that took over from football practice. Nobody was going to the pitch for a kickabout; few were practising the skills of the game away from arranged sessions. What were the youth and adult players doing? They were heading for the gym to make sure they stuck to a weights programme.

Wishing for days when half a dozen youth players set off for the pitch to hone their skills, may be a pipe dream. Celebrating their devotion to getting fitter and stronger is the way to go. It is a core development area but it can be fraught with danger. There are questions to be answered.

Does your club have gym programmes for players?
Are they aligned to individual needs?
Are they led/overseen?
Are players responsible for their own programmes?
Do players use the gym without supervision?
Does a qualified S&C coach have an input?
Is the gym equipment suitable?

If it's worth doing, it's worth doing the right way.

42
We need more role models to highlight the importance of proper nutrition and hydration.

More and more children are clued into who the top players are across our sports. We need these players to spearhead a *'nutrition and hydration'* campaign that resonates with the youngest players and their parents. What's consumed on a daily basis in a household won't change because of what a GAA player promotes or warns against. The family shopping basket is not the target….or is it?

Many clubs call parents' meetings to highlight different ways that adults can help player development. Among other things, the need for a balanced diet and consumption of fewer fizzy drinks is always mentioned. Some clubs bring in a dietitian or nutritionist and the professional slant can be a winner. However, it can also be a loser if the visiting expert baffles the audience with science.

Not too many years ago, the sight of a youth player carrying a water bottle was uncommon, to say the least. Now it's the done thing. Adult player awareness of the effects of carbohydrates, proteins and fats is so much better now. Being an example still counts. We just need to learn how best to promote it.

43
Video recording and analysis are no longer the preserve of adult teams.

We've had the county teams, then the adult club teams and now we've moved to record and analyse youth teams. Permission is given, documents are signed and the latest technology is ready to go.

It's easy to decry the use of cameras and laptops for youth games, but there's no denying that film helps us understand how players act on the pitch and film helps do away with storytelling in a lot of cases.

"He was inside the square before the ball was kicked."
"We lost five kickouts in a row, before their goal."

Of course, establishing facts is not the only goal of recording and analysis. Assisting with player development plays a very important part. Whether it be a series of clips sent to a player to be reviewed or a summary of chances taken/missed and watched at a team meeting, there are always things that can help with learning.

I have taken two valuable lessons from video work:
- A. Many players do not watch their own clips if these are focussed on improvement only.
- B. Clips played at normal speed are not very useful.

Having the ability to send match clips to a player within a day or two after the game, seems like a win-win. I'm not so sure these work unless there's a balance between positive and negative. The best I've seen have had an accompanying commentary (written or verbal) to direct the player towards specifics.

Even better have been those where actions in training sessions have been recorded, analysed and sent with commentary. I remember one example where a player was being easily evaded in tackle drills.

His clips showed how he took a long stride towards the ball carrier when that player shaped to go a certain direction. This left him unable to react quickly enough to the change when it came. Without the clips, he'd have been hard to convince that this was the root of the problem.

That leads nicely to my second concern; normal speed recordings. Those tackle/evasion clips were slowed to half and even quarter speed. The player was able to see clearly the effect of his step across and how his bodyweight shifted to a point where he was no longer balanced. Normal speed disguised it.

When match clips are shown to full squads during team meetings, they can be too long and they can also be too busy. Here are some things to consider:

Do you think players might only be watching to see if they appear on screen?

How easy is it for players to focus on a 60-second clip of game action and pick out what's important?

Last night I watched a recorded game. Early in the second half, a player got inside the opposition 45, passed the ball to a teammate and stood still. His direct opponent and two others raced towards the receiver, leaving the passer in open space. He took the return pass and scored.

The clip, at normal speed, lasted 7 seconds; double that when slowed. It took fewer than 15 seconds to illustrate…
…the power of doing nothing
…how easy it is for players to get drawn to the ball
…the effectiveness of one-touch football.

Short clips, slowed clips and specifics targeted. That's the way to go.

44
Let it run, let it run, let it run….respond.

Most definitely, there are coachable moments in every training drill or game…..but it's never a good move to address them all or even most of them. That's a bit of a statement to make, given that we never know how many will occur…so **all** could be two.

Agreed, but I'm talking about coaching habits here and one of our worst is to get in there with advice at every turn. We must deliberately practise how to watch for longer. What we presume to be things that need highlighted and corrected, may not even turn out to be problems; they may be blips. You may have read that sentence somewhere else in this book and I'm reinforcing it because it matters.

The final 10 minutes of a recent All-Ireland Club Championship semi-final had no fewer than 13 individual mistakes. Had this been a 10-min training game, there would have been an abundance of coachable moments….not too many for some coaches, but far too many for players.

One way to curb over-enthusiasm is to decide on a single focus for players in a short training game. If, during a competition game, you were taking notes and identified mistakes such as…

> *Poor first touch*
> *Running unnecessarily into contact*
> *50/50 passes*

…then it makes sense to present one of these to players as a focus in training, not just for an exercise but **for the whole session.** Team sport is littered with examples of coaches asking for too much too soon.

Be the player for a moment. The coach has just told your group that there are a few things which need worked on over the next while. He/she only names one…*first touch.* The focus for this session will be working on first touch and making it clean, as many times as possible. That's manageable. You are not going to ask what other things need work. You're going to play with a single focus.

Now you're the coach again. As you watch the session unfold, you make first touch your sole focus. Choose your coachable moments carefully. By all means stop the game to point out where a better first touch would have made a difference to a move. Even then, don't stop for every example. Let it run, let it run, let it run….respond.

45
Awkward but effective = leave it be.

I've had to change practice as the years have rolled by. Having worked with Terence and John on our *Head Hands Feet (HHF)* project, I found myself being drawn to the notion that there was one correct way to execute a basic skill of the game. My two colleagues were far ahead of me in both knowledge and adaptability, so I don't believe they were ever as rigid in their thinking.

Let me explain. HHF works a treat and is an excellent tool for identifying and practising what to do. If I take solo running as an example, HHF promotes...

Learning to look up and scan while running with the ball.
Dropping the ball from right hand to right foot / left hand to left foot.
Toe up rather than toe down to bring the ball back from foot to hand.
Straight leg rather than bent knee when playing the ball.

When players struggle with solo running, being able to observe and assist using HHF as a template can be a real plus for coaches. Yes, there will always be players who overcome obstacles without intervention from a coach, just like there will always be those who benefit from some input and welcome it.

What I was slow to recognise was the fact that some players can break the mould and be just as effective. In the case of solo running, this involved dropping the ball from left hand to right foot or vice versa.

I would immediately step in to correct this, my argument being that a cross-handed action left the player open to the ball being robbed by an opponent. A same-side action would protect the ball.

But what if that player was able to carry the ball smoothly and effectively and had mastered a way to protect it? He/she might be the only one in the squad able to do so, but there would be no denying that it worked.

HHF templates still apply in the vast majority of cases. It took me a while, but I have learned to recognise and welcome player idiosyncrasies that work.

46
If an engine isn't running smoothly…

Car trouble doesn't necessarily mean that there are multiple parts in need of fixing. One faulty component can have a knock on effect and be enough to determine how the vehicle runs. So it can be with a team. One player can be the difference between smooth running and a stuttering performance.

Take the following example from a leading club team a few seasons ago. Over a series of games, attacks had been characterised by a number of lateral and backward passes. There was nothing new in that. However, video analysis of the games showed that, while some were necessary, others were often taken with good options available ahead of the play. Further scrutiny of those passes let the coaches see that they were made by several different players; so, no discernible pattern it seemed.

This remained the case until they spotted that the receiver of many of these passes was the same player. His influence on attacks was huge. It was he who had been calling for the ball behind and adjacent to the play. A chat with the player, coupled with video evidence of attacking patterns, was all that was needed to change the dynamic.

One player…..one adjustment……more scores.

47
Supporting roles can be difficult to master.

Where to position themselves, when to run and where to run when a teammate has the ball; these are things that a few players can do well, instinctively, while others struggle.

I've already covered much of this in an earlier part of the book, under the title...***Making good decisions off the ball can be tough.*** This short section looks at more or less the same issue, but with a different eye.

Those who struggle may not be easily identified because they are hidden in plain sight. Coaches, like spectators, can find their attention drawn the immediate area around the ball. It's tough to concentrate on player habits off the ball, particularly if there is a considerable distance between the ball and the player in question.

A player's intention is, more often than not, to get hands on the ball and do something positive with it. When that player is ahead of a teammate who has the ball, he may be unsure of whether to **show or go.**

The **show** part is when the player runs towards the ball, wanting a pass. The **go** is an alternative. It's all about moving away from the ball to either draw an opponent further from it too or leave the same opponent far behind.

This is where training games can help a coach determine a player's support play habits. For these purposes, it's best not to count habits from low number games (eg 2v2, 3v3, 4v5) but to watch those training games which have numbers as close to competition-sized teams as possible (9v9, 12v12, 15v15).

That's when you get to see the balance between show/go and the appropriateness of each move, each time the player makes it.

A rule of thumb might be....if he shows for the ball more often that he goes away from it, it's worth making that player aware of the pattern and asking him to reverse the trend; ie reduce the number of times he runs towards the ball and choose wisely.

48
A slick training session may not be a good sign.

If your preparation for a training session ever gets to the point where you find yourself more interested in planning for things to run smoothly than in exposing players to messy learning situations, then the prep may not be worth it.

This is an easy trap to fall into, for the players we coach can be very complimentary when things are polished and well-organised on the training pitch. If you were a player who had just come through a session which moved seamlessly from drill to game to another drill and back again to game, you might well be impressed.

"That was good."
"Enjoyed that, thanks."
"Great session, lads."

These are comments often reserved for sessions packed full of slick football. You won't hear them after stop-start practices, where things were run and run again, in order to try and iron out problems or attempt to change habits.

Nor will you hear them when the majority of attacks in training games have foundered on the rocks of sharp defending and scores have been hard to come by all evening. Yet these messy sessions can be the ones where more learning happens.

From time to time it may be an idea to cut the prep to a minimum and start with a 15-minute game, involving all players. Place no constraints; let them play.

Management should spend the time observing play and discussing what unfolds. Keep one word in mind as you watch….*intensity.* If there is a perceived lack of intensity and both teams look good on the ball, there's something amiss. Everything after that 15-minute starter can't be allowed to stay the same.

49
Does the playing area suit what you want to do?

First off...I fully appreciate that many coaches have no choice here and must make do with what's given to them. It's not uncommon to have two squads training at the same time on the same pitch, each with a half or smaller to play on.

It's also the case that, despite recommendations from those administering Go Games (or the equivalent) in counties, some clubs have been known to fit as many mini-pitches as possible onto a full-sized one.

The latter move may be to maximise participation or to ensure a blitz is run off in two hours, not three. Whatever the case, the reduced pitch size is rarely matched by smaller numbers of players per team. It's hard to argue against giving every player the chance to be involved as often as possible, but we also have to guard against the game losing out.

Let me illustrate this with an example.
At an U8 tournament, the organisers set the pitch size at 40m x 30m. Each game is 7v7 and lasts 10 minutes. Expecting 14 children to play anything that looks like a game of Gaelic football inside such a small area is misguided.

Passing will morph into a mad scramble to offload the ball as teammates and opponents race towards the ball player. They've no distance to cover so they'll be on him like a shot. Either the dimensions have to be reset or the playing numbers reduced or both.

Back to the training situation again, where a club pitch is being shared by two youth squads. If you want intensity, particularly if you are keen to promote contact and tackling, you might choose to keep the area small and the numbers big; but if that's the format for all tackling work, you're not giving players opportunities to practise in the other spaces they'll have to deal with in a competition game.

In such situations, remember the value of dividing the group into three rather than two. A 15-min exercise, with teams W, X and Y playing a rotation series of 2-min games may serve your purpose:
W v X (Y observes)
W v Y (X)
Y v X (W)
Repeat all three.

Not only does the resting team get a chance to observe and discuss how to approach the next game, the brief rest also brings a freshness and places extra demands on opponents who have just been in a game.

50
To pass or not to pass….that is the question.

Often it is the case that players do not see passes because they have not been taught to see passes. Sometimes it is the case that coaches do not appreciate the difficulty of seeing those passes.

These two statements may be met with a collective furrowed brow from the coaching fraternity. Perhaps it's because few have ever thought about them. Perhaps it's because people believe it's an overcomplication.

For me, both are problems and both are linked.
We coaches can see potential passes because we are freed from responsibility and have time on our side. That means….we don't have a ball and we don't have bodies in the way. Add some elevation to our viewing position and we can probably see every possible pass that presents itself. Not so the player. Not by a long way.

A failure to appreciate the differences between player view and coach view can lead to us dismissing the idea that many players may need to be taught how to see passes. Only a minority will build their own understanding and knowledge through experience and self reflection. Many players need more.

A coach can't see the pass **for** the player, but the coach can help the player see that pass, either directly or indirectly. Here's one way to assist.

Look long is one of the simplest and most effective instructions for a coach to give a player who has just taken possession of the ball. Those two words, spoken before a training game rather than during it, push the player to look well ahead of his position to check if there is a teammate free for a pass or if a shot is on. If neither is an option, the choice is between giving a short pass in any direction or carrying the ball.

You're about to run a practice game and you want one team to practise looking long. You don't let the opposition know your intentions. A player asks *'What if we've just been defending and there's nobody ahead of me when I have the ball?'*

That's a valid question. Try not to answer it immediately. Ask the team to comment. The answer will come. *'Play the ball back and keep possession until we get people up there.'* Note...delaying the forward pass is only until people are in place. Moving the ball around is not ideal, but it's a means to an end. Even this little bit of information will help players learn the value of choosing the right moment. **Seeing the pass** is also about **seeing no pass** (and that isn't the same as not seeing the pass).

51
The days of feeding the ball into a 6v6 are gone.

Oh for a return to the good old days when a coach could stand on the halfway line with a few size 5s, wait for the backs and forwards to take their match-day programme positions and then launch the ball anywhere into the middle of the group. Three full backs, three half backs, three full forwards and three half forwards…all breaking from their perfect grid formation.

This harking after the good old days may come from more than a few coaches, but the truth is….that particular player formation is rarely seen nowadays. Having defenders and attackers practise from those positions is poor use of time.

A little bit of invention, with some help from video clips of games, will help. Use a mix of any of the following to make the exercise more realistic:

- Cut the numbers by at least two pairs
- Allow attackers to start wherever they wish.
- Overload one side of the pitch.
- Feed the ball from different positions
- Add a +1 to the defence
- Start with a 2v2 and add one player to each team once the ball is played

52
There's an attacking acronym to help with specifics.

SAID is an easy word to remember and an easy acronym to learn. Still, neither claim is a reason to use it. The thing about an acronym is that it can prove to be unnecessary or even pointless.

For me, SAID is one of those that works. It helps a coach study the detail of attacks and isolate different parts. When attacks break down, one or more of those parts may be the issue. Here they are:

S   SPACING
A   ANGLES
I   INCISION
D   DECOY

How is our **spacing**? Are any of our players running towards the ball carrier and closing his space? Who could move further from the ball?

What about **angles**? Do our inside forwards make runs directly up and down the attacking half? Are their runs giving ball players the chance to hit diagonal passes? Are runners ahead of the ball giving themselves a wide enough angle to see the ball and time when to cut inside from the wing?

Is there **incision** to our attacks? Are we regularly cutting through opposition lines? Is anyone playing incisive passes into the opposition half of the pitch? Can I see definite changes of pace from runners?

Decoy? Look for examples. Are players clearly making runs or holding positions to free up areas for teammates? Is there anyone not prepared to do that? Who is getting in the way?

Avoid the mistake of trying to look for all four of these at the same time. If the acronym serves to isolate important parts of any attacking system, then keep them separate when you study what's going on. Focus your eyes and your mind on one at a time or have other coaches take one each and report back.

53
If you feel you need to be vocal, try commentating instead of instructing.

There's an underage training game in progress and you are there on the pitch, either as referee or as coach. The play is end to end, a real mix of good play and unforced errors.

You're trying to be silent but you feel disengaged from the game. You still believe the players need you to be vocal, but you know you'll end up highlighting mistakes, instructing players and stopping the game at every turn. You begin to think these are your withdrawal symptoms, as you attempt to move from a lifetime of full instruction to observation.

Help is at hand. There is a step between the two that you may learn to like….it's called **commentary**. You don't have to mention every action on the pitch, just a few here and there to highlight good play.
Here are some examples:

It's the blues against the reds in this game….a real battle of the giants.

The reds are on the attack….good pass inside, but it's intercepted and the blues clear the danger.

A great move by the blue team. Clean first touches all the way to a score.

The blues switch the play with a super diagonal pass.

What a block by the red defender! Stopped a certain score there.

One touch football from the reds here. Not one ball carried into contact and so quick to get up the pitch.

If you can't see yourself getting immersed in commentary, then try short comments…..and keep picking out the positives.

Great score.
Super pass inside. Opened up the defence.
What a block!
What a catch!
Lightning turn.
Another great tackle.

The goal is to reduce instruction to a minimum and hand over more responsibility to players. Replacing it with commentary or with comments will help break the habit and, at the same time, reward players with positive affirmations.

54
Disciplined play doesn't only apply to defending.

Disciplined play....two words that conjure up images of a well marshalled defence, working to a plan and executing it with aplomb and with few fouls committed.

All of these things are true, but we have to start using same phrase about attacking. The challenge in this regard is to convince coaches and players that **disciplined play** is not synonymous with slow, measured attacking where a team's advance is held up and the ball is recycled back and forth across the pitch, while players look for that one opportunity to breach the wall.

It's more about learning to be disciplined at pace and when your players are marauding through the opposition half. It's about getting your **spacing** right when there's chaos and calling for passes and supporting players ahead, behind and to either side.

Players who pass the ball and run away from the receiver rather than towards or alongside; players who make support runs without narrowing the gap from 20m to 5m; players ahead of the ball who see the same gap closing and have the presence of mind to move left or right of the ball path and keep their distance.

It's these small things that add up to make an attack a disciplined one. Start work today.

55
And finally….adding to a library of stuff will never be as important as learning how best to use it.

"Despite the huge amount of discussion on social media about coaching styles and habits, coaches are still more inclined to engage when games, drills, scenarios and video clips are posted."

I wrote this on Twitter (@playergaelic) some time ago. I suppose it was out of concern that coaches appeared keener to amass games and drills than to reflect upon other aspects of coaching. Few coaches engaged and discussed topics such as game habits, delegating tasks, communication, sideline roles, the value of observation and the messy nature of learning.

The art of coaching seemed to be trailing far behind the need to stockpile resources. I had this image of a coach taking a screenshot of a drill or a game and running it on the same night in training, regardless of whether or not it suited. Even more worrying was the thought that someone might be running a game I posted, without paying any attention to the attached information.

An example:
There's a game called TWO-WAY MIDFIELD, where two teams are lined out with only **one midfielder** between them. That player wears a neutral bib and plays for both teams. The midfielder's job is to play for whichever

team is in possession. This gives the player more opportunities to practise how best to support forwards and defenders who have possession.

For me, it's not enough to just set this game up, choose a midfielder and run it. Coaches have to pay attention to what happens during the game and respond. That's why I added information on what to push:

> ➢ Encourage the midfielder to look for incisive, forward passes rather than lateral ones.
> ➢ Encourage the midfielder to scan the pitch to find the better positions to take up to receive a pass.

Around the same time, I added a different type of interactivity to my workshops. Previously, I would have presented an SSG to coaches and asked them to set it up, organise players and run it. I'd also have asked them to look for certain things as the game developed. Each team of coaches would have received a short list of questions. For example:

What do you see?
Do your attackers tend to run in a flat line or do some get ahead of the ball?
Who has worked out that kick passing is an option?
Are your players too narrow in attack?
What will your message be at the break?

This approach definitely promoted discussion among coaches as they watched, but it did little for feedback to individual players. I needed all coaches to engage with players and I wanted individuals to hear affirmations about how they were playing and to also hear how they might make improvements.

So began the practice of pairing coaches and individual players. The mentors could still discuss what they saw on the pitch, but when halftime came around (usually after five minutes of play), they now had a player jogging over to them, ready to find out what they thought about his/her game.

With a simple twist to observation and feedback, coaches were now becoming more clued into how they might use the game to watch individuals and learn more about their actions rather than just how to run it.

It's only my opinion and others may differ, but I feel we have to move coaching even further along this path rather than along one which is based on building a bigger library of activities.

Printed in Great Britain
by Amazon